My First Turkish
Animals & Insects

Picture Book with English Translations

Published By: My First Picture Book™

Ever Wondered How That Word Sounds?

We've introduced complimentary audio recordings for all our books to enhance your reading experience. Dive into the sounds at **MyFirstPictureBook.com** and not only read, but also listen and learn.

A Heartfelt Message from Our Publishers:

Your support does more than just buy a book. It uplifts native authors and fuels the dreams of a close-knit business. We value every reader, and your insights could shape our next bestseller! Got suggestions or feedback? Let's co-create magic. Connect with us through the 'Contact Us' section on our website at **MyFirstPictureBook.com**.

Ant

Karınca

kuh-rin-juh

Bear

Ayı

ah-yee

Bee

Arı

ah-ree

Bird

Kuş

koosh

Butterfly

Kelebek

keh-leh-bek

Camel

Deve

deh-veh

Cat

Kedi

keh-dee

Chicken

Tavuk

tah-vook

Cow

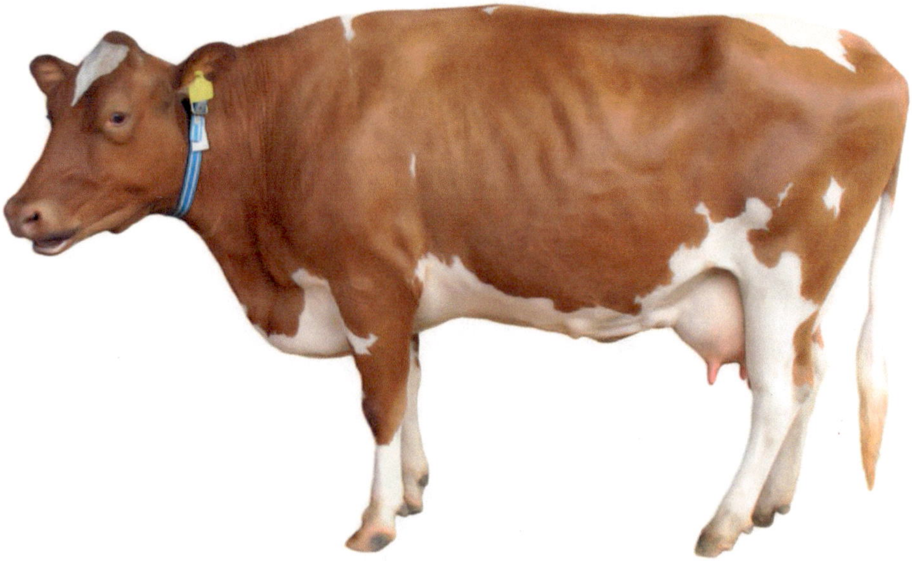

Inek

ee-nek

Crocodile

Timsah

tim-sah

Crow

Karga

kar-gah

Deer

Geyik

gay-yik

Dog

Köpek

kur-pek

Donkey

Eşek

esh-ek

Duck

Ördek

er-dek

Elephant

Fil

feel

Fish

Balık

bah-lik

Fox

Tilki

teel-kee

Frog

Kurbağa

koor-bah

Goat

Keçi

keh-jee

Horse

At

aht

Lion

Aslan

ahs-lahn

Lizard

Kertenkele

kehr-ten-keh-leh

Monkey

Maymun

mahy-moon

Mosquito

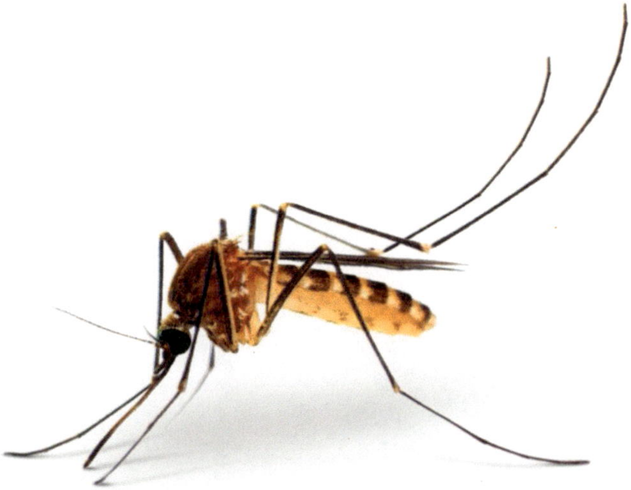

Sivrisinek

siv-ree-see-nek

Mouse

Fare

fah-reh

Pig

Domuz

do-mooz

Rabbit

Tavşan

tahv-shahn

Scorpion

Akrep

ahk-rep

Sheep

Koyun

koy-yoon

Snake

Yılan

yee-lahn

Spider

Örümcek

o-roo-m-jek

Tiger

Kaplan

kahp-lahn

Turtle

Kaplumbağa

kahp-loom-bah

Made in the USA
Monee, IL
05 November 2026

67375727R00024